Tony Granato

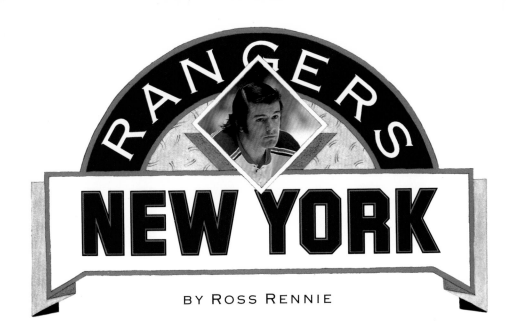

RANGERS

NEW YORK

BY ROSS RENNIE

CREATIVE EDUCATION INC.

Published by Creative Education, Inc.
123 S. Broad Street, Mankato, Minnesota 56001

Designed by Rita Marshall
Photos by Bruce Bennett Studios,
Frank Howard/Protography and Wide World Photos

Library of Congress Cataloging-in-Publication Data

Rennie, Ross.
  The New York Rangers/by Ross Rennie.
    p.   cm.
  Summary: A history of a Manhattan fixture since 1926, the New York
Rangers.
    ISBN 0-88682-285-8
    1. New York Rangers (Hockey team)—History—Juvenile literature.
[1. New York Rangers (Hockey team)—History.   2. Hockey—History.]
I. Title.
GV848.N43R46   1989
796.96'264'097471—dc20   89-37736
                                                      CIP
                                                      AC

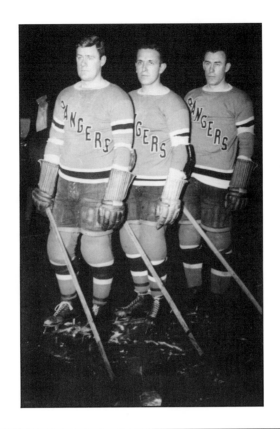

THE BEGINNINGS: 1926–1933

Ask people what comes to mind when you say New York City and you'll hear a variety of responses. Times Square, Broadway, the Empire State Building, the World Trade Center, Wall Street, the United Nations, Park Avenue, or Rockefeller Center. All of these sites are located on Manhattan Island, one of the five boroughs that make up America's largest city. It is estimated that there are over twenty million people in New York and the surrounding area. That makes it a prime spot for all sorts of entertainment. Devotees of the arts flock to Broadway plays and the

The New York Rangers joined the NHL in 1926.

The "third" Madison Square Garden was officially opened on December 25.

myriad of galleries and museums in the city. An incredibly large number of sports teams also call New York City home. They include soccer, baseball, basketball, football, and hockey teams. Another landmark of Manhattan is Madison Square Garden—home of the National Hockey League's New York Rangers.

Actually, the current Madison Square Garden is the fourth structure to bear that name and is located on the third different site. The original Madison Square Garden was named in 1879. Its name derived from the fact that it was located at Madison Square at Twenty-sixth Street and Madison Avenue. The original structure had no roof, and when problems with it became too great, a new building on the same site was constructed in 1890. In 1924, when the landowners decided to demolish the building, a new site had to be found. Madison Square Garden had become known as an entertainment center, so when the new building was constructed on Eighth Avenue between Forty-ninth and Fiftieth Streets, that name was retained. The new Garden was opened in November 1925, a year before the New York Rangers were formed. It was actually boxing promoter George "Tex" Rickard who, fascinated with hockey, was convinced that the game would be supported in the Garden. As a result, some folks referred to the new team as "Tex's Rangers," and the last part of the name stuck. Rickard hired Conn Smythe, who was already a success managing hockey teams in Toronto, to help get his new team organized.

Conn Smythe did not last more than a month before being replaced by Lester Patrick. Nicknamed the "Silver Fox" because of his white hair, Lester set out to build what quickly became an awe-inspiring club. This powerful new

The contemporary Madison Square Garden showcased the talents of Michel Petit.

The Rangers began their inaugural season by shutting out the defending Stanley Cup champions.

team was made up of two great wingers, the Cook brothers, Bill and Bunny. At center was the sparkling Frank Boucher, and on defense was the colorful Ching Johnson.

The New York Rangers played their first National Hockey League game on November 17, 1926 against the Montreal Maroons, a team that had just won the Stanley Cup. Very few teams can boast that they started as a club by shutting out the defending Stanley Cup champions, but that is what the Rangers did in their first game. The final score was 1-0 with Bill Cook scoring the lone goal.

That win was only the first of twenty-five that season, which would be enough for a first-place finish in the American Division. An outstanding achievement for a brand-new team. Hockey, as a result, quickly caught on as a popular sport in New York City. The New York Ranger games became the event to watch in those early years. The team was noted for the stylish clientele that it attracted to the Garden. Spectators were often seen in formal attire, and it was not uncommon to see Jimmy Walker, mayor of New York City, in attendance at the games. Although that first year the Rangers, with no play-off experience, were eliminated by Boston in postseason play, they had gained a reputation as both a powerful team and a class organization.

The following season, the Rangers did more than qualify for the play-offs; they defeated both Pittsburgh and Boston to gain a berth in the finals against the Montreal Maroons. But before the series could begin, a curious scheduling dilemma had to be resolved. For years the circus had come to Madison Square Garden at this time of year. No one had expected the New York team to make it all the way to the

Stanley Cup final. Although the circus was in the Garden when the finals were played, the conflict was anticipated. The long-term contract with the circus had to be honored. So the Rangers were forced to play their "home" games at the Montreal Forum.

If playing "home" games in the opposition's rink was not unusual enough, another strange incident occurred in this final series. With Maroons having won game one and with game two tied 0-0, the Ranger goalie, Lorne Chabot, was seriously injured and had to be taken to the hospital. In those days, the teams did not carry a spare goalie. When Lester Patrick asked Eddie Gerard, the Maroon coach, for permission to use Alex Connell, the Ottawa Senator goalie who happened to be in the rink, Gerard refused. Patrick was beside himself. He returned to the dressing room with the bad news. Jim Burchard, a reporter who happened to be in the dressing room, said, "Lester, why don't you put on the pads and play yourself." The real shocker came when Lester replied, "Okay . . . I'm going to do it!"

The game continued. Every Ranger was trying to keep the Maroons away from Lester. By the end of regulation time, the score was tied 1-1. In overtime the Maroons tested Lester, who had never before played goal. He held up. Finally, Frank Boucher scored to give New York the victory. They went on from that game to beat the Maroons three games to two even though they were outscored in the series 6-5. The Rangers had won their first Stanley Cup in only their second year in the league!

Coach Patrick and three players, Frank Boucher, Bill Cook, and Ching Johnson, eventually made their way into the Hockey Hall of Fame. They would be followed by many

1 9 2 8

The Rangers became Stanley Cup champions in only their second year in the league.

Like Ching Johnson before him, defenseman Brad Park was inducted into the Hockey Hall of Fame. (page 10)

During the 1960s and '70s, Vic Hatfield carried on the legacy of Frank Boucher.   11

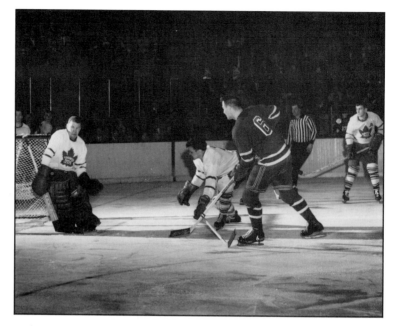

Like the phenomenal Bill Cook, Pete Conacher (right) was a talented offensive player.

other Rangers in the years to come. Incidentally, Lorne Chabot did return in goal for the New York team and over his eighty-game career with the Rangers allowed an incredibly low 1.61 goals per game. This still stands as the best record for any Ranger goalie.

The Rangers continued their fine play over the next five seasons, never finishing worse than third in the division. Each year in postseason play, they reached either the semifinal or the final series. Although they made it to the finals in 1929 and 1932, they were defeated by Boston and Toronto.

By 1933 only five players from the 1928 Stanley Cup team still remained with the Rangers. Those five, the Cooks, Boucher, Johnson, and Murray Murdock—all contributed to the second Ranger's Stanley Cup victory. And, just as goalie Lorne Chabot played a key role in the 1928 victory, so did goaltender Andy Aitkenhead in the 1933 series.

The finals were against Toronto. The Leafs had humiliated the Rangers just one year earlier. It was time for revenge. New York won the first two games handily.

Once again, of course, New York could not play all of their home games in Madison Square Garden. Why? You guessed it. The circus was in town, and hockey played second fiddle to the elephants! Game three, also in Toronto, was a tough match with lots of penalties. Toronto managed a 3-2 victory. The final game of the series was a goaltenders' duel. Lorne Chabot, the Ranger goalie in the 1928 series, now played for Toronto. Chabot and Aitkenhead fought it out.

Manager Lester Patrick and coach Frank Boucher joined their players in celebrating their second league championship.

Bill Cook was the only player who could penetrate either net. Cook had been the leading goal scorer for the Rangers for six of the last seven years. It only seemed appropriate that he would score the winner in this critical game. Even though it was in the midst of the Great Depression, the team got a champion's welcome by the city of New York. They were Stanley Cup winners again, the second time in their short seven-year history.

NEW BEGINNING, A NEW ENDING: 1934–1940

Only the very best teams realize that the time to begin rebuilding is when they are on top. Lester Patrick recognized that many of his players would soon need to be replaced by fresh, young legs. Patrick helped organize a New York Ranger farm club system that would help

Lester Patrick was named as the First Team All-Star coach for the second consecutive year.

provide future players for his team. It was these farm teams that produced the players that would give the Rangers their third Stanley Cup—players such as Bryan Hextall, Butch Hiller, Alex Shibicky, Phil Watson, and Lester's own sons Lynn and Murray.

Following their Cup victory in 1933, the Rangers began to rebuild. Somewhat surprisingly, there was not a big change in their results during the next three years. They qualified for postseason play twice, but missed the play-offs for the first time in the club's history in 1936. It is surprising sometimes how a team can seem to be weak and yet respond when needed. That was the story of the 1937 season. The club earned three less points than they did in 1936, yet qualified for postseason play. The Rangers were certainly not favored to win.

Their quarterfinal opponent was Toronto. In the two games, New York scored five goals, yet allowed only one. The next team they faced was the mighty Montreal Maroons. In this two-game set, the Rangers scored another five goals, and held the mighty Maroons scoreless. Dave Kerr, the New York goaltender, had allowed only one goal in four games.

Hockey was enjoyed by the folks of New York City, but the circus was loved. Once more the New York Rangers were forced, in all but the first game, to play their home-ice contests on their opponent's rink at a most crucial time of the year.

The Rangers faced the defending Stanley Cup champions, the Detroit Red Wings, in the finals. Behind the stellar performance of goalie Dave Kerr, the Rangers battled the Red Wings to the fifth and deciding game of the series before falling to Detroit.

Although he never won an NHL championship, 1960s star Rod Gilbert was all-time club leading scorer.

The next several years brought about a restructuring of the NHL. All the teams were consolidated into a single division. Also, the play-off format was altered. Only four teams would now qualify for postseason play. This new alignment seemed to favor the now-stronger New York Ranger team.

In 1940 the rebuilt Ranger club was at its peak. The team lost only eleven games during the regular season. The team defeated Boston easily in the play-offs and went on to win the Stanley Cup following a tough, six-game series with Toronto that featured two overtime Ranger victories.

That year was a great one for the New York team. Not

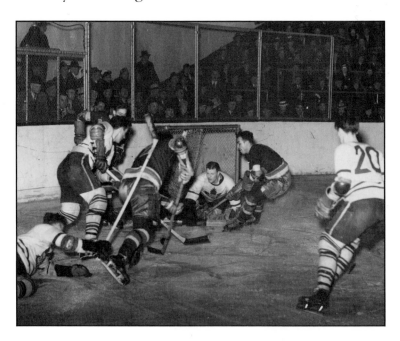

Forward Dutch Hiller (above) and his teammates (right) won the Stanley Cup in 1940.

Ed Giacomin's outstanding play in the 1960s and '70s was reminiscent of
1940 star Dave Kerr. (pages 18–19)   17

*New York began
a string of
unsuccessful
seasons that ran
through the early
1950s.*

only did they win the Cup, but they set some club records during the regular season. They established their longest undefeated streak of nineteen games. It may have gone longer except for a rather bizarre twist of fate.

In the twentieth game, the Rangers were down 1-0 as the third period drew to a close. The team had decided to pull their goalie if they had not scored with about a minute left in the game. Normally in those days, this move was made only when play stopped. New York decided to do something unique and pull their goalie while play continued. Lester Patrick, now general manager, happened to be on on the bench that night. He was unaware of this new plan and when he saw the six New York players on the ice, his yelling attracted the attention of the Chicago team. They took the matter up with the referee. Just as the Rangers were about to put the puck in the net, the referee blew his whistle to stop play. It should not have been blown. But the play had been stopped, the surprise was over, and the winning streak came to an end. It was a great strategy, discovered by a great team, which has been used successfully by many teams since then.

DECADE OF DISASTER: THE 1940s

lthough in 1941 and 1942 the strong Ranger team managed to finish their regular season reasonably well, they did not perform well in the play-offs. In the following years World War II had a large impact on the club as the Rangers lost many of their top players to the armed services. In fact, no team lost more key personnel than the Rangers. This was apparent in the poor records posted by the team. They never got to the Stanley Cup final for the remainder of the decade.

Coach Frank Boucher could do little to improve his club's dismal record.

The lowpoint occurred only four years after they had won the Stanley Cup. In what was now a fifty-game season, the 1943–44 team won only six games. They ended up with a dismal seventeen points for the entire season. It was the second year in a row they had missed the play-offs. This streak continued for four straight years. In each of these years the Rangers ended the regular season in the sixth and last spot, well out of play-off contention. From 1943 to 1947, they.were the worst team in hockey.

One season the team went twenty-five games without a victory. Things were so bad that the one-time great New York star Frank Boucher, now the coach, inserted himself in the lineup. To Boucher's disappointment, he performed better than many of his regular players.

With the war finally over, the Rangers could begin a

rebuilding process once again. Many of the stars of the game now returned from the war effort. Improvement was slow at first, but the team could go nowhere but up.

The Ranger farm teams, established over a decade earlier, brought more good players to the island of Manhattan. Chuck Rayner was the New York goaltender during this period. Only two Ranger goalies played in more games than Rayner over the history of the team. They were Ed Giacomin, a star goaltender from the mid-1960s to the mid-1970s, and Lorne "Gump" Worsley, who took over the goaltending duties from Rayner in the early 1950s.

In addition, there were three centers who helped turn around the New York team in the late 1940s. They were Buddy O'Connor, Edgar Laprade, and Don "Bones" Raleigh. It was the goal-scoring ability of these players that finally helped pull the Rangers from the depths of despair and make them a respectable team once again. In 1948 the team finally put together a good enough season to finish fourth in the league and qualify for play-off participation. Although they lost in six games, the series was close. Considering the lack of any play-off experience on the team, the Rangers could be proud of their efforts.

The decade ended with the team slumped back into the last place in the NHL. However, the future was not as dismal as one might think. The Rangers ended the 1949 season only ten points behind the Toronto Maple Leafs, the eventual Stanley Cup winner. The talent in the NHL had become more balanced, and the teams were more even than in the past. With a few changes, the New York Rangers could look forward to lots of play-off action.

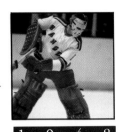

1 9 4 8

Only goaltenders Ed Giacomin (above) and Lorne Worsley appeared in more games than Chuck Rayner.

Phil Esposito's play during the 1970s was even more spectacular than that of his 1940s counterparts.

BOOM TO BUST: THE 1950s AND 1960s

Ed Giacomin became goaltender, following in the proud tradition of Chuck Rayner.

Suddenly, during the 1949–50 season, the pieces began to fall into place for the Rangers. Every shot that in the past would have deflected off the goalpost seemed to fly directly into the net. Rayner, at the top of his game, received able assistance from forward Pentti Lund and Tony Leswick. With a big improvement in the team, the Rangers managed to grasp fourth spot in the NHL. The Montreal Canadiens were first on their play-off agenda, and in five games the series was over. New York had defeated the Canadiens and their star Maurice "Rocket" Richard.

The Stanley Cup series against the Detroit Red Wings went a grueling seven games. Detroit emerged as the victors with a double-overtime win in the deciding game.

After the contest, Sid Abel, the Detroit team captain, came into the Rangers' dressing room, a most unusual action for an athlete who had just won a championship. He walked over and shook Rayners' hand and congratulated him on a great performance. Then he turned to the other Ranger players and said "Don't you guys know when to quit?" It was the highest compliment he could pay.

It would be more than two decades before the Rangers would reach the Stanley Cup finals once more. To say the rest of the 1950s and 1960s were a disappointment would be an understatement. During that period, the New York Rangers failed to qualify for the play-offs twelve times. When their record was good enough to get them into postseason play, they always lost their first round. It seemed as if someone had put a jinx on the team.

To give you some idea of how lackluster their play-off

efforts were in those days, you need only look at the play-off rounds against Montreal. Four times New York met the Montreal team in a seven-game series. Twice they were shut out completely, and in the other two series New York could only manage one win. Needless to say, lots of changes were made. Throughout this period, the longest-standing goalie in Ranger history, "Gump" Worsley, was their thankless net minder. It wasn't until 1964, when the dynamic Emile Francis took over as coach, that Worsley received help and the rebuilding of the team began in earnest.

Rod Gilbert, destined to become the club's all-time leading scorer, recorded ninety-seven points.

A RETURN TO RESPECTABILITY: 1970–1987

In 1971 the Rangers did something they had not done in over twenty years—they won a play-off series. The victory brought them up against the Chicago Blackhawks in second round. But Chicago, with great goaltending and the phenomenal scoring power of Bobby Hull, proved too much for the Rangers that year.

The play-off experience of 1971 helped virtually the same Ranger team make it to the Stanley Cup finals the following season. This was the first time in Ranger history that the circus did not interfere with Stanley Cup final "home" games. Oh yes, the circus was in town, but now the arrangement was different. After the elephants were put to bed, the new Madison Square Garden could put ice down in a matter of a few hours. However, playing on their home ice was not enough for the Rangers, who bowed to Bobby Orr and the mighty Boston Bruins.

The New York Rangers made it to the Stanley Cup finals only once more in the 1970s and not even once in the

John Vanbiesbrouck's outstanding play established him as one of the 1980s' premier goaltenders. (pages 26–27)

John Vanbiesbrouck won the Vezina Trophy as the best goaltender in the league.

1980s. In 1979 they put together their best play-off bid in recent times. After easily eliminating the Los Angeles Kings and Philadelphia Flyers, the Rangers faced their crosstown rivals the New York Islanders. Although the Rangers prevailed, the hard-fought six-game series left the team with little stamina to face the Montreal Canadiens in the finals. The Canadiens, who had not faced tough play-off competition, had an easy time with New York and won the series in five games.

The New York Rangers would make the semifinal series twice in the 1980s. In 1981 the Islanders beat the Rangers on their way to their second consecutive Stanley Cup. This "other" New York team would go on to win four Stanley Cups in a row, meaning that in their short history they had won the Stanley Cup more times than the longtime New York team, the Rangers. In 1986 the winners of the semifinals against New York, the Montreal Canadiens, were also the eventual Stanley Cup champions. Even the heroics of Vezina Trophy-winning goaltender, John Vanbiesbrouck, were not enough to stop the relentless efforts of Montreal.

TODAY'S NEW YORK RANGERS: 1988 AND BEYOND

Looking toward the 1990s, the team was loaded with talent. With the likes of Swedish stars Ulf Dahlen and Tomas Sandstrom, as well as right wing Brian Mullen, the Rangers had a lot of scoring punch. At center and left wing, the Rangers seemed to balance experience and youth with Paul Cyr, Dan Maloney, Lucien Deblois, Kelly Kisio, Marcel Dionne, Jan Erixon, and Jason Lafremiere. However, more depth would be needed at these positions.

John Vanbiesbrouck continued his superb play in goal, and Bob Froese provided capable assistance. The only other area where some maturing was needed was in the defensive corps. They had some quality performers, including Ron Greschner, James Patrick, and Normand Rochefort. Those that needed more experience but had great potential were Michel Petit and David Shaw.

The Rangers' hopes for future success brightened considerably with the additions of Brian Leetch and Tony Granato in the 1988–89 season. Teammates on the 1988 U.S. Olympic hockey team, the rookies made a major impact on the club. Leetch, a first-round draft pick, gave the Rangers a defenseman who was also capable of a potent scoring attack. With the combination of his offensive and defensive skills, he was even being compared to Bobby Orr.

"I saw Orr at the same age, and I put Brian in the same breath with Orr," said former Ranger general manager Phil Esposito. "I've never done that with anyone."

Granato, a fiesty forward who could fill any position on the front line, was as adept at scoring goals as at killing penalties. Because he was just five feet ten inches and 185 pounds, some had wondered if he would be able to compete in the NHL. But he quickly answered his critics with his aggressive style that combined speed and strength.

"What good is size if you don't use it? I know a lot of 6'4″ guys who don't have half Tony's heart," said John Vanbiesbrouck.

With the additions of Leetch and Granato, the team was poised for the future. It has been about fifty years now since the New York Rangers have won the Stanley Cup. Nonetheless, they have a long and exciting history. More

1 9 8 8

James Patrick's offensive talents blossomed as he led all Ranger defensemen in goals, assists and points.

29

Forward Tony Granato became a rookie sensation in 1989.

Brian Leetch won rookie of the year honors in 1989.   31

than thirty former Rangers have been elected to the Hockey Hall of Fame and many more will be added in the future. But the only thing the New York Ranger fans want is to break the jinx and see their players once more sip champagne from Lord Stanley's Cup.

1 9 9 0